# in the midnight hour

ISBN: 978-1-7357944-2-6

GODS&RADICALS PRESS

Layout by Gods&Radicals Press

For bulk, solidarity, and wholesale copies
please contact us at
distro@abeautifulresistance.com

See our other books and online journal at
ABEAUTIFULRESISTANCE.ORG

# *within*

# we heal when we feel our guilt

## witnessing as healing, as vengeance

Once, a person I saw as a mentor hurt me. Our relationship had begun in a friendly, amiable, affirming way, but over time the relationship began to feel coercive and pressuring. Wanting to protect his feelings, I gently refused and expressed discomfort when he asked things of me I did not want to do, and in response he said the right things, but his actions showed my boundaries would not be respected. The situation felt intolerable, particularly as a person who easily sees the best in others and has a tendency toward people-pleasing to avoid conflict.

When we were about to spend time together, I would rehearse the ways I would stay centered and focus our interactions on what I liked about our relationship, but in person I felt my boundaries and concerns dissolving under the very skills and expertise that I wanted to learn. Walking away, I felt good and told myself I was okay with everything that happened, but within an hour I would fall into anxious nervousness, shame, and wondering how to avoid this happening again. A part of me saw him as holding an enormous charisma that overrode my will, and it was hard to shake though I used every tool I could. Every tool except for telling others what was happening outside of my closest people.

Eventually I broke off contact, but later ended up with this mentor in another shared community space. I told myself I would be fine, but I felt wracked with shame and a quavering sense of terror every time we inadvertently made eye contact or had to speak.

With the support of my therapist, I began telling my story to others. This validation of the ways I'd been manipulated helped me to ground myself in recognizing that what was happening wasn't okay, and to see how much I had been doing to protect this person's feelings at the expense of my own.

A confluence of circumstances created the opportunity for the two of us to have a facilitated confrontation. It was the kind of restorative justice process that is dreamt-of and so hard to accomplish.

We showed up, and the facilitator was both skilled and aware of how power skews what seems like a neutral relationship. I told my story, and the facilitator met my ex-mentor's deflections and dismissal with firm, kind accountability and encouragement.

As I watched, I saw my ex-mentor's countenance start to soften, and tremble, as his defenses against pain relaxed and he began to feel his guilt and shame over what happened. At the same time, I felt my own heart lighten as I became unburdened of all I carried. I walked into the process trembling in fear, and walked away feeling joyful, light, and free. There was no more for me to carry, no desire for further retribution, nothing.

The seed of vengeance may simply be in the longing for having one's hurt witnessed and validated by the person who caused us harm. An instinctive knowing that this could bring healing and relief. But so rarely are those who have caused harm able to bear the feeling of their own guilt and shame. Instead they defend against it, minimize it, reject it, or compel others to hold it. Lacking that outlet for healing witnessing, vengeance becomes that venomous instinct to cause them a hurt that will match the hurt we feel, escalating rather than healing discord.

## what we want and what we owe

Perhaps the fear of guilt is that it aligns with a sense of obligation which is greater than the gratification of our own wants and needs. The feeling invites us to reckon with the conflict between others' needs and expectations and our own desires.

So much goes back to power and its uses. Guilt is that which weaves us into just and beloved community. Guilt knits communities together, and it may be wielded abusively by someone with power and authority who feels threatened by the needs of another. We may give a gift out of love, and then use that gift as a hook later when we feel angry or scared, as a way of coercing the person to take care of us.

Guilt may be an inner prophet who calls us out when we're out of integrity and need to make amends. It is appropriate to feel guilt for committing, participating in, or allowing harm or injustice to occur. Guilt spurs us to make things right and grow as people. Yet those who cannot tolerate guilt may demand forgiveness as though it's owed to them, and crumble when it's not given. Such a demand asks the harmed person to do their emotional work for us, rather than letting us suffer and work through our own guilt.

Meanwhile, many of us have been trained not to allow others to feel guilty, ashamed, or in pain. We are all too ready to spare them their guilt and remorse, consoling ourselves with a story about our strength or virtue. Forgiveness may be granted before the offense is even known. When we hesitate to take on the pain ourselves, we feel our own pang of guilt. We may tell the story that by letting them be accountable and feel their guilt, we are torturing them. Yet all we are doing is letting them feel their own feelings.

Ironically, in those moments, if everyone involved was willing to simply practice feeling their own guilt and allow each other space, there would be greater healing than the urgent efforts to fix and shut down pain.

As animals who crave connection, we seek it through its many guises: approval, love, sex, enmity, vilification. At times it does not matter what the connection is, whether it feels good or awful, so long as it exists and we know we exist. Shame, however, is an emotion of disconnection. It is the emotion that tells us we have been severed from the group and are in danger of death, social or otherwise.

As we've learned thanks to Brené Brown, Shame says, "I am bad," while Guilt says, "I've done something wrong." Yet in our flattening, moralizing way, the overculture of the United States collectively believes that only bad people do bad things, and therefore to feel guilty is to prove the story of shame. This is to our detriment. We are all capable of causing hurt and harm, and likely will at some point in life. When we cannot tolerate the guilt and repair process of hurting another, our hurting tends to escalate. Defenses against feeling guilt render us more indifferent to others' suffering.

In a cyclical model of time and development, metaphors of spiraling and pendulums are useful for contemplating how growth occurs. We turn into one direction until we've gone as far as we can, until it begins to hurt and impede our growth, and continue curving to the other side of the polarity.

One possible journey: We experience pain when we've hurt someone in the process of following our own desires, and start feeling a sense of guilt whenever a "selfish" impulse arises. Over time, however, we find ourselves hemmed in by guilt and always prioritizing the wants and needs of others from that feeling of obligation, setting aside parts of us. Eventually we feel the chafing of making ourselves smaller for the comfort and satisfaction of others, and reject guilt, shame, and obligation in favor of prioritizing ourselves.

Another possible journey: We see the smallness in the lives of people around us who submit themselves to relationships that look painful and loveless, and vow to put ourselves first. We deny and refuse anyone who expresses hurt or upset with us, fearing the loss of autonomy and control, until one day we hit a limit. Perhaps we feel utterly alone, with no one special in our lives. Perhaps we are held accountable in a painful and undeniable way, that fantasy of independence shattering when the harm we've caused finally catches us. Eventually we begin listening to that guilt and longing for connection, learning how to remain ourselves and respect the needs and feelings of others.

We reach the edges and continue curving back, each oscillation becoming more refined and skillful. Soon those vibrations seem almost invisible from the outside as we gain greater mastery and inner complexity, learning we always have a range of responses to every moment, and each response offers a gift and a limitation.

## *autonomy and intimacy*

So long as we treat emotions as things done to us or injected into us, we allow ourselves to be under the power of others. At the same time, we are capable of feeling others' feelings and taking them into ourselves, and experienced and instinctive manipulators know how to find the people who will do this for them. In the swinging between autonomy and intimacy, we have all we need within us to practice discernment between what to give and what to retain.

Start within. Start breathing and imagine you find the core of aliveness, the belly center that gathers in your vitality, your passion and will, the core in which the fires of life burn. This is the center that has been with you since you were a feral child taking pleasure in the brightness of the colors of the sky and grass, disgusted with the textures of food, who played and kissed with innocence. Sense how that is in you today.

Imagine you find the core of relationship, the heart center that gives and receives social connection, that feels the web of relationships and your place within it, that senses how others feel toward you and you toward them. This energy reaches out into your environment with breath, communicating yourself into the world, and draws that connection back into yourself as guidance. The emotional field is the field of relationship, and this is the center that knows how to navigate this realm. Sense how that is in you today.

Find the core of potential, the head center that receives knowledge from the visible and invisible worlds, that gathers it into the cup of the skull and filters it through the nervous system. Here is the throne of that which we may call the higher self, the deep self, that which can see further and broader and deeper. That which sees the bigger picture, sees what is possible, that can bring us into radical, intentional, and beautiful action. Sense how that is in you today.

Imagine a circle around you that contains all you know yourself to be, all that is your responsibility. Imagine that as a cellular wall, a membrane, a fence, a bubble through which we can take in what we need and push out what does not belong to us.

With this connection, let us return to guilt and shame. That connection of the fires of the belly, who knows my innate worthiness, and the chalice of the head, which can see further, helps us to look at the matters of heart and connection with more discernment, self-compassion, and dignity. Without the head and the belly, those ruled by the heart center may be wholly subsumed by concerns about others' opinions and approval.

Too often feeling guilt causes us to crumble and feel as though we must utterly abase ourselves for forgiveness or reject the accusations of harm. Again, guilt bound to shame, a combination that says "I am bad because I did something bad." When this story is alive, we feel our worthiness and capacity for future happiness are based on the forgiveness and opinion of the person we've harmed. Which, you might think would make us more inclined to be kind to them, but more often than not elicits all the defensiveness, denial, controlling, seducing, and further gaslighting that only compounds the harm.

Let your guilt be here fully, in your sphere. Let yourself know that no one owes you forgiveness or the opportunity to make amends. This guilt belongs to you, it is telling you who you are and what you are capable of. More importantly, it tells you who you want to be. What does your guilt say to your belly? Your heart? Your head?

When we struggle with harming others we can feel at a constant impasse. "I want to be better but I keep fucking up!" We may get anxious and overwhelmed, afraid our friends and family will get exhausted by our failures and walk away from us. What we may not recognize is that it's our avoidance of guilt and defensiveness that is the most alienating. The capacity for forgiveness is quite expansive when the guilty person demonstrates genuine remorse, contrition, respect for the hurt person's healing process, and commitment to change.

All of this is helped by simply feeling our own guilt, before doing anything about it, and while we work to make amends. Pain spurs us to change, and guilt is a pain that says what we are doing is unacceptable. We have no reason to grow when we assuage, avoid, or numb our pain.

Those who have been harmed do not owe—and cannot be expected to provide—kindness. Some may be able to offer kindness, which demands even more energy to protect and support one's own hurt. Pressuring someone to provide forgiveness or kindness to assuage your guilt only compounds the hurt and slows down the outcome you want. Better to slow down, express remorse, and give the hurt person the space and power to determine how they want to interact with you in the future, what they want from you.

In the meantime, we can work on listening to the lessons of our guilty feelings and continue to grow and live our lives. It is impossible and unwise to stop living entirely while processes of accountability unfold, but it is useful to get support from a class, a community, a support group, or trusted friends and mentors to help us work through our conflicting thoughts and feelings and figure out what boundaries are appropriate. Even better if these supports are not people who unfailingly take our side and tell us we've done nothing wrong, but who help us to sort through our behaviors and figure out how we can do better.

## *finding our place within collective and ancestral legacies*

I grew up a white person in a country built upon the myth of the supremacy of white people, and lived in a Midwestern state that at one point actively embraced the politics of the Ku Klux Klan. So I was surrounded by explicit and implicit racist thought and action, some of which I recognized. Yet even when I actively rejected white supremacy, I was not fully aware of the extent to which racism informed my words and actions. When my friends of color started to push back and call me out, I did not respond graciously. I made it harder on them. I dismissed their experiences or focused on my own feelings rather than acknowledging the hurt.

Over time, I realized those who called me out were acting in self-care for themselves and respect for me. They cared enough about themselves to not let me be a shithead around them all the time, and they cared enough about our relationship to invite me to work on it and change rather than walking away. Many, I suspect, did walk away.

Listening to my guilt rather than defending, taking time to stew on my feelings and try to see things from their perspective, helped me to radically reorient my humanity. I aspired to be a person who is kind, just, and in integrity, and guilt showed me how far apart was the distance between that ideal and the ways I'd been practicing relationship. It continues as a spiral process of progress, regression, curiosity, discovery, hurt, regret, and accountability.

Most of us living in the United States who are not one hundred percent Native or the descendent of enslaved people owe our existence to the forcible taking of land, property, and personhood of others. We benefit from hurt that continues to live in the bodies of the descendants of those harmed, in the inequities of policing, income, wealth, and access to healthcare, clean water, food, and safety. Yet those that benefit most from this wonder, "Why should I feel guilty?"

If I were given a beautiful painting, and then learned that painting had been stolen from someone else, that would be a complex ethical issue. Perhaps I myself did not do the crime, but now I know the crime has been done and harm exists, and I have an opportunity to participate in rectifying it or continue perpetuating it. To admit that we do feel guilt means knowing that our pleasures and eases have been paid in blood. We confront in stark terms the depths of conflict between personal comfort and satisfaction and that which we owe to others.

# unknotting the bindings of toxic guilt

To feel guilt about causing harm is a healthy and productive emotion that leads us into healthy, self-responsible relationships. Without guilt, we would have no sense of ethics, no concern for the harm done to another person, no capacity for intimacy. Guilt tells us when we've fallen out of integrity with our values, and it leads us back to self-respect.

Unfortunately, guilt sometimes also serves to bind us in automatic deference, to make ourselves smaller, to sacrifice our needs and deep values for the comfort and well-being of others. Guilt makes us vulnerable to control, and at its worst makes us controlling of others.

When we feel responsible for all of another persons' feelings and needs, any action we take that makes them uncomfortable, upset, or inconvenienced begins to bring up feelings of guilt. One person's disappointment in me feels like a direct assault on my sense of self. I have to avoid it at all costs. That is when guilt becomes toxic and oppressive.

## *strategies of control and dominance*

If I cannot differentiate others' feelings from my own, it's inevitable that I begin to figure out strategies to manage or avoid feeling guilt. Often this comes out as efforts of control. I must manage myself so that I never hurt, anger, disappoint, or grieve another person—which quickly becomes overwhelmingly stressful, surrounded by people with wildly different responses. I might also try to control those around me so they don't have those feelings, through bullying, placating, flirting, lying, double-dealing, or exploding in response to any kind of accountability.

To be in a healthy relationship, I need a clear sense of my self, my edges, and the edges of the other person. I need enough distance from their feelings and behaviors to soothe and know myself, so that I can meet them authentically. When I fear disappointing someone, I lack the distance to think about on these expectations. Who appointed me the job of keeping them happy? Is this what I honestly want, or something I'm doing to avoid bad consequences? Is this a task I gave myself? Are the expectations to which I hold myself, or to which they hold me, ones that I can live with?

Perhaps their expectations, hopes, and needs are fully valid but still not correct for us. In the early stages of a romantic relationship—okay, in nearly every stage of a romantic relationship—these differences in expectation become clear. Our partners get upset at us for behaviors that are innocuous to us. Imagine two partners: Elisa and Jacob. In Elisa's family, you ate whatever was in the fridge, but in Jacob's family you never eat the last of anything without asking. Both expect this behavior of their partners because it's normal to them, not realizing that family cultures are different. Then they clash, because someone has to be right. Eventually, perhaps, they arrive at the point of seeing these as different and equally valid beliefs, and find a compromise that works for both.

But if Jacob reacts with intense anger and shaming every time Elisa finishes something without asking, and Elisa feels guilty and believes she's in the wrong, both become smaller and disempowered in the relationship. Elisa starts walking on eggshells, not sure what will set Jacob off. Elisa feels uncomfortable even asking Jacob what he's upset about, thinking that with Jacob she should simply know and understand and something must be wrong with her for not getting it.

Jacob's anger might run from a deeper wound. Perhaps he expects that Elisa should be able to know his desires without him needing to ask for them. He feels embarrassed about having wants and needs and shy about asking for what he wants. When Elisa does not magically know what he's thinking, he feels a deep, years-old disappointment that he is invisible and unseen. While Elisa could spare him from this by being accommodating, in the long run it might be necessary for Jacob to feel this disappointment as his own. Until he begins to face how much this pattern of expecting his needs to be known without him asking for it, he will continue to feel disappointed, disempowered, and heedless of how much he sets up his partners to fail.

Rather than accepting responsibility for others' feelings, I can focus on cultivating my ability to respond. This is separation that enables connection. Rather than internalizing another's opinion of me as something threatening and needing control, it behooves us to work on making our inner experience a safe place to experience all of our emotions and thoughts.

When it's okay to feel disappointed, hurt, angry, fearful, or joyous, it's easier for me to realize that other people can have these feelings without dying. And, indeed, maybe these feelings are necessary. Nobody's feelings are "wrong," they are information. When a person feels betrayed by my actions, that's important information for them in deciding what they need to make this relationship work. If I feel remorse for my actions, that's important information for me about what I'm willing to do to repair the relationship. If I feel that I was acting in integrity, that is information too.

Without this differentiation, we feel as though we should and must control someone else's emotional experience. We feel bound to their feelings, that any upset or anger they feel toward us is another binding that keeps us from being ourselves or doing what we want. We have to stop everything and fix them, even if we don't feel we did anything wrong. We feel reluctant to share our perspectives and act. While this is primarily for our own comfort, to avoid the feelings that come up when there is anger or hurt directed toward us, it becomes a hook. This person's disappointment, anger, or hurt develops its own power of control. Unconsciously or otherwise, the relationship becomes a struggle for dominance.

## *liberation from guilt and oppression*

Here is an important truth, emerging from social justice discourse: "You are responsible for your impact, regardless of your intent."

Here is another important truth: "I can only be responsible for my experience."

While paradoxical, both truths are valid. I like to joke and throw out random witticisms in conversation. When I'm lucky, people laugh. Other times people respond with irritation, upset, or anger. My intent was to have fun, my impact was that the person became upset. I might have made light of a topic that is sensitive and important for the person. I failed to meet them where they were, I took up space when they needed it, or I poked a sore spot. When I was younger and stupider, my humor had racist and sexist overtones. Even when I thought I was satirizing racism, the Black person who didn't know me and didn't need to hear that felt upset.

My impact did not line up with my intent. To know this is a gift. It helps me to think about what went wrong and how I can better align the two in the future. In the meantime, it is worth acknowledging that I caused harm and make amends.

Where privileged folk—white middle to upper class people in particular—get stuck is in toxic guilt. When we're confronted or called out, we are in the dilemma discussed above. We do not fully understand the harm we caused and want to keep it at a distance

Being ruled by guilt is not healthy for anyone. It is stressful and narrowing. Marginalized people often experience pressure to contort themselves for the comfort of the socially, politically, and economically powerful, that the feelings of the powerful are more worthy of care and concern than their own. This reinforces fragility in the privileged, who do not have enough practice tolerating emotional stress. In these cases, the consequences of the marginalized not doing emotional labor for their oppressors tend to be more costly than feeling bad for disappointing someone.

In this writing, I speak of "marginalized" versus "privileged" as relative positions rooted in how much social power one has. Young children are less powerful than their parents. Employees are less powerful than their bosses. In the United States, immigrants, Native people, and people of color are generally less powerful than white people.

The current moment of #metoo is rife with questions about guilt and expectation. As stories come into the light, we see more clearly how much the subjects of patriarchal violence have had to endure, swallow, and allow to poison themselves to get along. Now is a moment when the anger has broken this pattern of denial and minimization. Women and other victims of sexual assault, coercion, and harassment are sharing their stories and pursuing action.

Speaking out is behavior that toxic guilt would normally inhibit, and we see that guilting rising to meet the outpouring of anger. Repeated injunctions to think about the harm they may be doing to the men they are accusing. Redirecting the conversation to looking at how those who experienced the harm might have taken more responsibility to avoid it or stop it.

Privileged people struggle, I think, to step out of a dynamic of dominance and submission with regard to feelings. There is a sense that someone's feelings have to be right and another's wrong, so a white person working on being "woke" may look at being called out as a sign that they need to throw out all their feelings and perspective and wholly embrace the truth of whomever is calling them out. Complete submission, which is rarely asked for nor appreciated.

My observation is that part of this is that dominance in relationship is so ingrained that the privileged person is unable to see the difference between engaging in honest conflict versus defensiveness or stonewalling. A person early in interrogating their own perspective gets feedback on their defensiveness or stonewalling and then assumes that means any kind of disagreement or difference of opinion with a person of color is racist.

Men regularly told they are "mansplaining" are unable to fully understand the difference between that and having a conversation. This naturally engenders some frustration which then leads to demands for emotional labor from the marginalized person.

As a white man, I've gone through phases where I've been called out by a woman or a person of color and responded with a conciliatory, "Thank you, I'll go think about it," response that did not engage the critique and mostly seemed to leave the other person feeling grossed out.

These days I practice staying in the conversation, staying with the discomfort and trying to understand what is being said to me while also standing in my perspective and experiences. I am in a place where I do not automatically agree with every person who calls me out or challenges me—but neither do all women or people of color agree with each other. One thing that I do believe, however, is that these folk know better about what it's like to live their experience than I do. There is something I can take in from their perspective that would enrich mine, even if I don't agree with everything they say. And as I want to move toward my liberation, I would prefer to support others in seeking their own liberation and not thinking I know what they need to do.

As I explore my relationship with guilt, I find there is not a clear maxim that will guide me through each interaction gracefully. Nor do I want a carceral model in which acknowledging guilt results in exile or imprisonment. What I seek is a way of working with guilt that brings justice to those harmed, reconciliation when possible, and liberation for all involved.

Having an emotional experience has material consequences for our ability to concentrate and be present in the world. If you've ever felt anxious, angry, or triggered, and tried to read, take a test, or do your job, you've likely seen how much your emotional state affects you. These consequences are mediated by how many inner and outer resources we have to experience and process the emotions without getting overwhelmed. We can deliberately harm someone by pushing their buttons, triggering them, lying about what's happening, being defensive, being hostile and insulting, or going cold and not responding at all.

The Restorative Justice movement employs strategies such as group sharing of stories and experiences to process the harm of a crime and lead both the perpetrator and victims of the crime to find a workable resolution. This model inspires me in its integration of healing and justice for both victim and perpetrator. I believe such a process would further help us to discern who is guilty but capable of returning to the community from those who lack conscience or remorse and will not respect community agreements. For such people, whether on a social or interpersonal level, we do need the capacity to set and defend our boundaries.

## *working through hurt without someone being wrong*

When I explore patterns of toxic guilt with clients, we often find deep wounds arising from childhood experiences in which disappointing, hurting, or angering one's protectors and caregivers was experienced as a life-threatening risk. Children depend so much upon their caregivers for emotional regulation and basic needs of existence, and sometimes our experiences of learning are such that people internalize a belief that it's literally dangerous for a person to be angry or hurt. This becomes a vulnerability in the psyche that activates even as adults when we are better equipped to deal with whatever life throws at us.

Stepping on an emotional landmine or triggering a trauma response are circumstances in which the paradox of "I am only responsible for my experience" and "My impact is more important than my intent" come into play. The person who is experiencing the trigger or emotional upset may want to blame their partner, but this leaves them disempowered and dependent upon their partner. The partner who stirred up trouble may want to dismiss or blame their partner, but this would be unhelpful and make the problem worse.

It is a difficult dance, but understanding this is our partner's personal struggle empowers us to be more compassionate and emotionally supportive. When I am not struggling with my guilt and shame, I have more room to be caring and understanding, to acknowledge how they experienced my actions. I don't have to agree with their interpretation of reality, but I can understand it.

In relationships, these kinds of negotiations are frequent and necessary for a healthy system. Perhaps

Jacob tells Elisa that she's allowed to do whatever she likes on her date with Rhonda. Then, say, Elisa decides to spend the night at Rhonda's since it's getting late, and texts Jacob the information before turning off her phone to go to sleep.

Jacob suddenly feels betrayed and angry. On some level he expected Elisa to come home after her date, and maybe he was not fully conscious of that expectation until now. Perhaps he thinks it's "obvious" and that Elisa deliberately crossed a line. When Elisa comes home, thinking she's been abiding by the "do whatever you like" rule, she suddenly finds herself being angrily insulted or berated for breaking an agreement that was never overtly made.

If Elisa feels a sense of toxic guilt, she might then stop seeing anyone and start resenting Jacob, because he's so inconsistent. Or she might start hiding, skirting rules, or demanding legalistic rules and insisting Jacob cannot be upset if she follows the letter of the law.

Jacob could have handled things differently. Perhaps her coming home is actually not that important to him, it's that he felt taken off guard by her texting him right before going to bed. Perhaps it touched on some old pain of his, fears of abandonment. Perhaps this experience has caused him to realize he does have a need to have Elisa home at night, though he's otherwise okay with her doing anything else.

A way he could communicate that would be to own his experience and share it. "When you did this, I felt angry, hurt, and scared. I think I need you to come home at night, or I would prefer if you had called me so we can talk about it and not you deciding and then turning off your phone." Instead of internalizing guilt over his feelings, Elisa could acknowledge his experience and feelings and share her own. "We had not talked about it, so I assumed it would be okay. I didn't think I was going to stay until we found out how icy the roads had gotten."

In this conversation, harm happened but no one did anything "wrong." Both partners find a solution through understanding what happened and their own feelings. If they create a rule now, it will be one that works for both—"I will call if I want to spend the night," or Jacob will realize it isn't that important to him after all, he mostly wanted some reassurance that she considered his needs.

Safety and mutual accountability are necessary in working through these situations of guilt. Each person involved needs to have the relational safety that it's okay to discuss their experiences and feelings about the event without being judged, shut down, shamed, denied support, thrown out, assaulted, or otherwise attacked. Each person needs to have the inner safety that it's okay to experience all of their feelings—especially the painful ones—and to be honest about what they understand of their motivations. Each person needs to be willing to hear and say things that might be difficult.

This accountability is deeply helped by speaking from and of our own subjective experiences. We cannot control our partners, but there are many ways we can talk of our feelings and needs that decrease the friction within the conversation.

It helps to set up rules, such as one person shares their experience while the other person simply listens, quietly, without making a noise, giving commentary, or making faces, only asking for clarification and understanding. Then the other participants get their turn.

Rules for talking are as important as rules for listening. One thing that seems to engender the most defensiveness and anxiety is when one person makes accusations of the other. "You did this, you made me do this." We're all walking around in our own subjective worlds, privy to our own inner thoughts, feelings, and motivations, but only able to at best make an informed guess about another person's. Most of us hate being misrepresented, too, and feel an urge to defend ourselves against any kind of impugning of character.

One strategy to defuse this is to focus on naming your observed behavior and then speaking of my experience. "When you sent me a text saying you were spending the night, I felt angry and hurt. I tried to call you, and your phone went to voicemail, so I figured you'd turned it off. I wondered if you were upset with me. I had a hard time sleeping, and I felt scared."

For those of us with toxic guilt, these conversations may bring us into a deeper level of affect, the part of us that fuels the patterns of guilt and social control. We may feel terrified, for example. Rage. Some primal emotion connected to a childhood wound, an experience we've been trying to avoid since. Scared of being punished. Scared of being abandoned. Enraged that our needs were unmet, or ignored. Feeling that is an opportunity to plant our feet on the ground, feel the steadiness that meets them. Breathe deeply, imagining that you can give space to those big feelings, that you can become big enough to hold them with ease. And then we get through the conversation and find that the worst hasn't happened. Or perhaps it did, and it wasn't so bad. Something needs to change, but our adult selves are able to manage it. We learned something deeply important that we've needed to learn to keep growing. We showed up and were held to account, and now we can be more conscious, more effective.

## *the path of transformation*

Here people begin to have some discomfort. "What if we make a rule, or set a boundary, and my partner continues to break it?" The discomfort connects with deeper fears around addressing toxic guilt. What if we are truly honest about ourselves, and our partner cannot accept it? What if we stop placating or accommodating? What if our partner feels betrayed by our actions, and we have to admit we caused harm? What if I stop doing everything for my community, and our event fails because no one else stepped up?

Essentially: "If I stop controlling others, how can I control them?"

To be empowered, we must accept responsibility for our thoughts and feelings, and let go of the idea that we can control others. To stop saying "you made me angry" and start owning "I felt angry." "You made me feel a feeling" binds you to me, and me to you. I have to make you different so I can feel differently.

I've noticed a backlash to this wisdom, but I believe the backlash is to the abuse of this wisdom. Too often folks conveniently twist this insight to dismiss and belittle others for daring to have feelings. "You need to be responsible for your feelings." That truth needs to be balanced by the truth of "I am responsible for my impact." Feelings are valid sources of information about my needs and values. Anger tells me that I have a boundary you've crossed, or a need going unmet, and that needs to be addressed. My responsibility is to explore the feeling, figure out what need it's pointing toward, and communicate that to you in a respectful way. If you think my responsibility is to never feel or express anger or hurt, you are welcome to go fuck yourself.

If we set a boundary or express a need and our partner persists, then we've learned a lot about what they're capable of and what kind of relationship this is. You get to decide what to do with that information. You get to decide if you are safe to stay, and what you need to create more safety for yourself. You might have to find resources and allies. You might have to make some hard decisions.

This is often scary, and feels unfair, but it is the cost of personal power and freedom. When we accept responsibility for ourselves, and stop trying to control, we have so much room for greater honesty, deeper intimacy, more authentic alliances. If another person's guilt tells them they are out of integrity, then they have all the motivation they need to do the work of coming back to you, working with you to repair.

We are bound to unsustainable patterns out of a fear of death. Not the death of our bodies, but the death of a way of life that is familiar to us, reliable, known. We can fear it like we fear our mortality, for too often we prefer the known misery to the unknown. To change our relationship to guilt will lead to other changes. Maybe the event fails. Maybe the relationship ends. Maybe people do step up and we find the community is able to hold us. Maybe the relationship deepens and becomes better than we'd ever imagined. Maybe things end, but we find something even better.

# *for the people whose caring entraps them*

There are people who will use the best of you against you.

There are people who will receive all the love and strength from your healing heart and still reproach you for not having more to give.

There are people who will look to your integrity and say you are at fault for their harming you.

There are people who will flail and cry out that no one's helping them while their erratic movements push away your outstretched hands, draw out your kind and patient direction, draw you into the water beneath them.

You are the strong ones, the competent ones, the

rocks, the mothers, the fathers, the warriors, the nurturers, the caregivers. You are the ones without whom "everything would fall apart."

And that is a truth that is also a lie that keeps you trapped. You who learned to set aside your wants and needs, to shelter your vulnerability while caring for everyone else's, you have learned to believe the well-being of those around you depends on you.

You have learned, through disappointment, not to expect much of others. You have learned that your plate can only be filled after everyone else has had enough, only to find others took more than their share and there is not enough for you.

You have forged an identity around this suffering, a self-righteousness that is poor compensation. Your Self has been buried beneath the mighty weight of obligation, a burden you cannot help but carry and others seem all too willing to avoid.

If you are the only one "keeping it all from falling apart," then "it" should not be together.

We need you to stop doing our work.

We need you to let us struggle more.

We need you to stop saving us at the expense of your joy, to stop resenting us for the burdens you are unwilling to put down.

We need you to let us grow strong enough to carry our own weight, by no longer letting it weigh you down.

We need you to learn from our neediness, to finally tend your heart and draw the circle around its home. To know that no one's wants and needs are rational, and yet they are worthy of care. To know that your wants and needs are worthy of the care you give to us.

We need you to stop resenting us for giving more than we give back. We need you to match your giving with what you receive.

We need you to know your limits and abide them, and not yield to our incompetence, our pleading, our helpless desperation, so that finally we will learn the secret.

The secret you have always known: there is no one who knows the right thing to do. There are only those willing to accept the consequences of doing.

We are in the last days of the age of emperors and martyrs. Now comes the age of radical community, of interdependence, of one precious and irreplaceable Self in community with others, equal in worth and dignity.

# disappointment is a spiritual experience

Once, I was in a situation where my lease was ending in one city, and I'd be moving to another city soon, but I needed a few more months before I was ready to move. One of my relatives lived nearby, and I called to ask if I could stay with him a few months. He declined, explaining why he felt his space wouldn't work for me, but out of my mouth spilled an acidic, "that's disappointing."

Later, another relative called to make sure I was okay and not mad, sharing that my words had unsettled the relative who wouldn't house me. That was when I realized that saying I was disappointed was one of the sharpest arrows I could have pointed at my relative, and that I'd always known this on some unconscious level. Now I tell myself a story that on that side of my family, to disappoint another is one of those unspoken things one does not do.

Which, simultaneously, made the threat of being disappointed a highly successful piece of leverage for manipulation. I remember one year there was an event my grandparents and the rest of our family was attending that I'd decided wasn't interesting to me. I received a birthday card in which my grandmother wrote, "So disappointing to hear you won't be joining us." Almost immediately I bought my plane tickets to go home for the event. That weekend, at dinner with my grandparents, I mentioned this to her. "You knew exactly what you were doing," I said, and she smiled at me with all the gracious humor of an elderly Irish American woman who had won.

While I began to notice the foundational role disappointment played in my personality, it wasn't until years later that I saw how deeply afflicted I was by the fear of it. I was sitting in my spiritual community as we dealt with the aftermath of our founder retiring from teaching and leading us. We were engaging in a conflict, and I realized I felt both resentment and body-shaking fear.

I could sense a scared part of me, saying, "It's all going to fall apart!"

I could sense a guilty part of me that felt, "I have to do something to keep us from falling apart." That part of me truly felt if I did nothing I would be a disappointment to others, and blamed for the community's collapse.

I could sense an obligated part of me wanting to volunteer to take on more tasks and make it work.

And I could sense the part of me that felt deeply resentful of the whole group and burnt-out. That part said, "Why isn't anyone else stepping up? Why is it always me?"

In that moment I saw a pattern of movement from Fear to Guilt to Obligation to Resentment. They nested within each other like Russian dolls, with Fear at the core and Resentment as the most recent layer. Everything in my life had begun to feel like an obligation, and thus sapped of joy. Whenever someone wanted something of me, I felt afraid of hurting or disappointing them, and either felt obligated to do it or tried to find a passive aggressive way of avoiding it. This relation extended even to my own desires, which quickly became tedious "to-do" items as soon as they were recognized.

With no reprieve, no inner permission to take a break, no sense of safety and trust in others to hold things together, my life had become permeated with resentment. Going home, I realized I even resented my dogs for wanting attention and care.

The threat of disappointment was the unnamed ruler of this state of affairs. As long as I kept pushing and holding things together, I imagined no one could be disappointed in me. As long as I was too busy to know what I really wanted, I would not feel disappointment.

Yet seeing resentment appear told me this pattern had become a death sentence to my soul. It was telling me I was way past my limits and not doing what brought my life meaning. Because I was terrified to say no, resentment was stepping in to alienate me from my perceived sources of obligation.

The cycle failed me and the people I loved. When I thought that sense of obligation was righteous, it deprived my community from the opportunity to take responsibility for itself. And without considering, I kept pushing what I believed the community needed and resenting them for not stepping up, instead of seeing the flow of energy as a sign that the community did not need what I pushed.

Though it terrified me, I started practicing saying no to obligation and stepping out of responsibilities. I started to decide it was okay if things fell apart when I stopped holding them together. If it depended solely upon me, then it was not sustainable. If it truly needed to exist, others would help. Over time, my relationships have grown stronger, I have witnessed my community rising to take on the work, and I have learned that I am still lovable even when I have boundaries. I feel calmer, happier, and more loving because I have permission to take the time I want to nurture myself and my interests. My boundaries are stronger and clearer as I become more familiar with my limits and needs.

And I find myself disappointed from time to time.

Disappointment is a co-walker on the spiritual journey. Those of us who come alive with visions of the beauty and potential of humanity, of the richness of nature, of the joys of the body or the exaltation of the soul, of the transcendent experience of loving and being loved, eventually have an experience in which our experience falls far short of what we'd expected.

The spiritual vision is always in tension with material reality. Yet our practices call upon us to accept this world as it is, the soil in which we plant our beautiful, inspiring dreams and visions.

Perhaps the worst disappointment is when we do experience exactly what we dreamed of, and then it falls apart. The dream job turns out to be filled with backstabbing, busy work, and leadership who undermines every constructive effort. The time wasn't right for love to blossom. Seemingly random forces ate away the foundations of joy. The person we thought was the love of our lives turns out not to be who they said they were. Or they were exactly who they said they were and we weren't listening. We experience betrayal and manipulation by our revered spiritual leaders. We discover our best was not enough, or learned too late we took for granted something that needed more loving care.

Disappointment occurs when we become conscious that our experiences do not match our expectations. When we cannot tolerate the feelings of disappointment, we'll engage in our favorite avoidance strategies to stave it off as much as possible. In part, we sense that disappointment could crush us and spiral us into depressive meaninglessness and nihilism. If this experience was so crushing, then why try again? Why open ourselves up to more hurt?

Yet both avoiding and being crushed by disappointment begins to make us inflexible. If we tend to blame ourselves for our suffering, then avoiding disappointment results in routinized action, sticking with the known, avoiding risks, and detachment. In a sense, we live lives of perpetual low-grade disappointment because we never consider or pursue what we want.

If we tend to blame others for our suffering, then avoiding disappointment results in blame, anger, cut-off, refusing responsibility for our expectations or behaviors, and looking for a new object of desire without having done any self-reflection. In a sense, we live lives of sporadic, intense disappointments because we keep thinking we have what we want in this new object, but not learning how to discern whether it's an appropriate object.

Neuroscientist Jaak Panksepp identified seven core emotional systems that exist across species. One that he called "SEEKING" is one of the most primary, and it is the experience of excitement and anticipation that drives us to pursue what we want or need. This system is, in a sense, without specific object, and in another sense attaches to several objects. SEEKING arises when we need to look for food, or a partner to mate with, and may be implicated in our experiences of longing for more abstract desires around family, career, and spiritual enlightenment.

One suspicion I take away from learning about Panksepp's work is that SEEKING is a pleasurable sensation that drives us toward what we imagine will make us happy, but in a sense it can never be satisfied. Once we get what we want, we are no longer engaged in the pleasures of anticipating it, hoping for it, imagining how it will be to experience it. We are instead dealing with reality, and reality is never as exciting as the fantasy. It was the experience of SEEKING itself that infused the desire with feeling.

This understanding of SEEKING reminds me of the Buddha's Four Noble Truths, that all existence is suffering and the cause of suffering is craving. SEEKING may be a construct describing the fundamental nature of craving that informs our animal psychologies. Even when I am fully satisfied and have manifested everything I want, that part of me will become dissatisfied from disuse and cause me to desire something new. Yet if I were to shut down that SEEKING altogether, I would become depressed.

When we allow ourselves to experience disappointment and grieve the expectations we had, I believe we refresh and refine our SEEKING system. We gain more clarity on what it is we truly want and need. Our expectations become more workable. We may stop seeking a spiritual community of perfect harmony and freedom from human flaws, and start appreciating how our spiritual frameworks help us make sense and work through the experience of simply being flawed humans. We may stop seeking a partner who knows our every desire before we do and start appreciating a partner who simply washes the dishes before being asked.

To disappoint is not always a sign of having done something wrong. There are times when others appear to have expectations we didn't want or don't agree to and there is no way to set a clean boundary without disappointment. It was not wrong, for example, for my relative to tell me I couldn't stay at his place, and might have been better for our relationship in the long run rather than him taking me in with resentment. Neither was it wrong of me to admit that I felt disappointed, though I suspect I could have been less bratty about it.

Telling the truth of our feelings and experience brings adjustments in our relationship. If you need me to be a certain kind of partner and I am unable or unwilling to do so, it is wise to move away from me. If you value the relationship more than the expectation, working through our expectations will likely let us come closer together. Whether the expectation or the relationship is more important tells us a lot about ourselves and each other.

Some of us will go ahead and do our best to meet those expectations even if we don't really like them —we may not even know we're able to question or disagree with the expectations. Authoritarian leaders expect, and expect their expectations followed, often when they've failed to even articulate the expectation. Those who experience authoritarian parents or leaders learn to intuit and uphold expectations and, depending on how deeply ingrained they are, may even think the leaders are always right and trustworthy in their expectations.

Permissive parents and leaders, in contrast, may have few expectations or avoid conflict by not acknowledging when they have expectations. Yet those who experience this style of leadership may find expectations communicated in oblique, confusing ways that cannot be clearly named and discussed. A child may realize they've disappointed their parent somehow, sensing frustration or distance, but not have any language to understand and discuss it.

An authoritative style of parenting and leadership would identify and name clear expectations and, if those are disappointed, talk through what happened that got in the way of the expectation being met. Perhaps there was a failure of communication and understanding, a circumstance, or perhaps the expectation was not correct for the situation. Authoritative leadership negotiates accountability and disappointment to make expectations fairer and more workable.

Remember that at the bottom of Pandora's box was hope. When we avoid opening up our box of expectations and airing all that shit out, we lose the possibility of hoping for an experience that is more aligned with what we want. We open up more space for a different, fiercer, more enduring, earthier truth to emerge.

# boundaries invite intimacy

After reading Cristien Storm's excellent *Empowered Boundaries: Speaking Truth, Setting Boundaries, and Inspiring Social Change,* I've been thinking about my own boundaries and exploring boundaries with clients.

Storm does such an excellent job laying out the merits of boundaries, obstacles to them, and a simple but flexible framework for identifying and enacting boundaries that I'm going to recommend you read the book instead of offering a lot of my own thoughts. But one thing that I've been thinking about a lot is that boundaries are as much about connection and intimacy as they are about safety and separation.

Robert Frost wrote, "Good fences make good neighbors." There's a complex truth in that. Separation allows for connection and greater intimacy. It is scary and uncomfortable to realize everyone else is inhabiting unique subjective and equally valid worlds.

A fence demarcates the line between us, reminds us that we are separate and have separate experiences. A fence reveals the limits of my territory and responsibility, and helps me to focus on cultivating the kind of experience I want to have. I can only care for what is within my territory and you can only care for what's in yours. If I want to raise a beautiful garden and you want to pave your land and install an Olympic size pool, those are experiences we can have, but if the construction from your pool begins to harm the environment of my garden, we need to have a conversation. I can be accountable to what I've done, and give you feedback about how you affect me, but I am still only able to tend my land.

But a fence is not a wall—it is open and permeable, it allows for connection and exchange. Building a wall to shut out everyone around me means losing access to important information, resources, opportunities for alliance. The land does not truly belong to any of us, and we all affect and are affected by each other in our relationship to that land. The fence helps me to have focus on what is within my capacity to tend. I cannot tend the entire land, but I can tend my own territory.

My own tendencies toward conflict and boundary-setting have historically been avoidant, with certain notable times I would set boundaries and would experience them being ignored or overridden as though I'd said nothing at all.

That's a story I tell about myself but it's also not entirely true. As I write this, I remember a time in high school—when I was perhaps most fearful and inward—when some random people at a campsite approached me claiming that I'd stolen and destroyed their Confederate flag during the night. Though I was scared, I was surprised by how strongly I stood my ground and told them they had no proof and should leave me alone.

(In retrospect I imagine myself saying "I wish I had ripped up your fucking flag!" There was no reason for them to be flying that flag which wasn't steeped in white supremacy. We were in Indiana, which fought for the Union. But I don't think those words actually came out of my mouth. They were a group of older guys who looked in better shape than me, and I was meek enough.)

As I've deepened my work around my own needs and boundaries, I've learned how much avoiding boundary-setting is its own form of hiding and inauthenticity. For so long I thought it was good to be a person who was easy-going and bad to be a person who got angry or expressed disappointment. I remember adults commenting on how polite and patient I was when people behaved with disrespect toward me, and I built my ego structure around that praise.

But after a while, I realized it was a lie. The disrespect affected me, and mentally I was fully aware of the people who hurt or disrespected me. Instead of addressing it with them, though, I outwardly behaved like everything was okay—reassuring them it was fine—and then would emotionally distance myself. No one knew I was upset, but then people also didn't know if I cared at all. The distancing manifested as simply withdrawing and not communicating with them, not making further plans, or getting really awkwardly controlling about future plans. At worst, I would find myself doing my innate power move of being really intellectualizing and criticizing the person from a "rational" perspective.

These defenses are very effective at both avoiding conflict and quietly ruining important relationships. There is behavior punishing a prior transgression, but the punished person does not know what they did that was upsetting and has no opportunity to correct it or make amends. It also did not require me to take ownership of how I participated in the problem by not stepping up and clearly communicating my wants and needs.

In the past several years, I've been learning to tell my important people when I feel hurt, angry, or disappointed, which has felt awful and scary and embarrassing but also made so many of my relationships better.

Setting a boundary communicates that I care about something, reveals myself to the other person. Indeed, it often communicates that I care very much about the other person. That I cleared my calendar to make plans with you tonight and it hurts that you let something else take priority. That I want to be present when I hurt you but I feel flooded and overwhelmed when you raise your voice and criticize me instead of talking about your feelings. That I want us to be closer, but when you dismiss or ignore my feelings I feel shut down and sense myself emotionally moving away.

These are not punitive consequences, things I am saying or doing to hurt you, these are genuine expressions of my experience for you to consider. If you want to keep going in the ways that cross my boundaries and cause these consequences, then I need much firmer and thicker boundaries. If you want us to be closer, you'll notice the consequences and respect the boundary.

# practice and fighting with humans, not enemies

When the wooden sword cuts toward me, I reach mine out and catch the impact, gather it close, and then open for the next attack. We are practicing a simple exercise of stepping forward, cutting, and my receiving the attack without harm to either of us. My partner is newer. Where I've been practicing for almost two years, I've only begun seeing them around in the past six months. Not the biggest gap in experience but enough that I can recognize both the eagerness, insecurity, and tension mirrored in his attacks.

"Can I offer you a suggestion that helped me?" I ask.

I'm hesitant to offer advice or corrections since I still feel like such a beginner, but today I feel the urge, and he's open to it. "Don't look at the swords when you strike. Look at me. It's weird, but it helps."

He's open to it but seems mistrustful of his ability to try the advice, and I get it. My instinct has always been to stare at the perceived imminent threat, tension building in my body. An internal fight wants to occur when I see the threat coming—the sword cutting toward my face, the melting ice caps, the erosion of protections of women and queer people, the increasing polarization. One part of me wants to turn rigid, feeling safer, as though by becoming tense my body will absorb and negate the damage. Another part of me wants to completely collapse in cynicism and despair—resistance is useless and laughable, there is nothing to be done but watch the destruction.

Practicing a martial art is one of the ways I've learned to notice and step out of that battle. Learning to calmly receive a sword blow teaches me much. When I stare at the sword, too much of my mind is active. I am hyperfocused on the threat and my beliefs about the threat. My body tenses and doesn't know what to do. It's like all my focus is in my brain, on the thought of being in danger. When we're driving and we become hyper-focused on something dangerous—an accident on the side of the road, for example—our bodies begin to subtly start to move toward it. It's a strange paradox of the human threat response system, to move toward the feared outcome.

But when I am gazing at the person attacking me, eyes soft, taking in everything that is happening, my body feels more engaged and able to respond. In part I see that I am not in danger. I am practicing with another human being who instinctively does not want to hurt me, especially when we're looking each other in the face. We are connected. Humans have an instinctive aversion to directly causing harm to another human, it's something that has to be trained out of us, or else we have to be convinced other people aren't humans, depending on the reason we are being encouraged to kill and harm.

In the Tarot, Swords represent the realm of thought, intellectual processes, and analysis. The suit of swords tends to be a rather gloomy, painful affair, full of grief, indecision, paralysis, and conflict. Yet my first Tarot teachers spoke of the capacity of the sword to "cut through the bullshit."

When we are too fixated on our thinking, on our certainties, and we focus too much on each other's swords, then we lose that capacity for discernment and cutting through bullshit. Our fighting is about whose ideology is the most correct, the most pure, the most evil. We stop seeing the human on the other side, holding the blade, and then we lose a great deal more. So much damage occurs when we forget about humanity. We create restrictive laws that create suffering for real people. We hurt the people we love most because we are fighting against an imagined monster.

Instead of fighting enemies, I like the somewhat antiquated word of "adversary." An adversary is simply one who is on the opposing side, a person who challenges me, who brings attention to issues I wasn't considering, who points out the holes in my logic, who provokes me to understand my position in a deeper way.

In life, this feels deeply threatening, but if we can look at our adversaries and remember their humanity, perhaps we have the possibility of simply practicing together. At the same time, it is not merciful to allow myself or others to be harmed if there is anything I can do to defuse and end the attack.

After two years of practicing martial arts, and more than fifteen years of practicing sitting meditation, I am beginning to find I have enough expertise to be very clear about when I'm doing things wrong. In my dojo, the teachers often say the expression, "Perfect practice makes perfect," and I feel a sense of despondency at the belief that my body has not learned all the skills necessary to even engage in perfect practice.

Yet I see that now I can feel when the movement is not working correctly. I am beginning to sense the corrections I need to make instead of needing people to point them out to me all the time. I still encounter the judgment and expectation that, during sitting practice, one is supposed to be able to entirely clear one's mind of all thought, and I find those moments exquisitely rare.

Attachment to perfect execution or perfect outcome seems to me another way of setting myself up for rigidity and despair. What has been far more workable for me is a goal of becoming better at returning to center, as my teacher T. Thorn Coyle often taught. When I am knocked to the ground, I have learned how to fall gently and safely and get back up, ready for another round of practice. When I find myself mired in cynicism and despondency, it takes me less time to remember myself and recommit to my work.

There is no end to work or the cycles of history, though practice helps us begin to see that what we encounter are not cycles but spirals. Instead of circling through the same issues and problems in the exact same way, we begin to notice how this iteration of the cycle feels different, more expansive. We see more nuance in the problem. We spend less time being stuck in the outcome. The damage is less severe. We find more capacity for joy even when these problems exist.

May we all show up to practice together.

# supporting your strong people: some suggestions

A friend of mine recently made a Facebook post that went viral about checking in on your strong people, or your "rocks," that resonated with a lot of people. I can't speak for all "rocks" but I have some thoughts that might be useful for those unused to thinking of their strong people as needing support.

Your strong people need support.

They may not ask for it or show it. You may think they are inhuman or don't have feelings. But they are human and they feel.

Often strong people have a deeply rooted instinct to put others' needs ahead of their own, with a concurrent doubt that others will be available, able, or willing to support them. Strong people might have a long history of feeling failed, ignored, or humiliated by the people who cared for them, so they learned how to care for themselves.

It is a strange paradox that these very independent self-caring people are nevertheless often driven to be available and helpful to others, and struggle to say no. The unconscious belief might be something like, "Once everyone is okay, then I will take care of myself." Which never happens.

For those who are not used to offering support to your strong people, I wanted to offer some suggestions:

## *be assertive but not pushy*

Reach out and ask how they are, then after a few moments of small talk, ask how they really are. If they say they are fine and don't need anything, or push you away, let them know you are available and willing to be there for them.

Avoid digging or asking a ton of leading questions, unless you know your rock well enough to ask what you know is the right question. The more you seem to want information or emotional revealing, the more suspicious and withdrawn your rock might become.

## *be open to anything*

Sometimes when your strong person opens up, you won't even realize it. "I didn't have anything in my fridge today and had to miss lunch." Okay? Not the end of the world?

But you may not understand the context—how important it is to them to eat regular meals, the sense of security they feel in opening the fridge and finding food. How this is an indicator that their routines of self-care have gotten lost, and how this symbolizes their sense of failure, overwhelm, inadequacy, and fears of slow decline. You don't have to get all that right away. The takeaway is: keep in mind that the problem might feel a lot deeper than it seems at first.

On the other extreme, your rock might open up to you with some mind-blowing unexpected shit you couldn't have predicted or even imagined they would be involved with.

And it is entirely possible that they would say either or both in the same tone. Like it's not that big of a deal, maybe even kind of silly.

You might laugh. Laughing a bit is not a deal breaker. But once you get that this is important, try to compose yourself quickly and invite more information.

Do not, however, make fun of the problem, or imply that it's not a big deal. In that case you might be confirming their secret fears that their problems are unimportant or no one they love can take care of them. You will lose the opportunity to support them and likely will not have another for a long time.

## *stay focused*

Once your strong person starts opening up, don't check your phone or shift your focus on other priorities. That might be experienced as a sign that you are uninterested, overwhelmed, or think their problems don't matter. They may quickly clam back up and continue pretending things are okay without telling you how you affected them.

If you do need to shift your focus, be really up front about it. "Hey, I need to use the restroom but I want to keep listening to you, so I'll be right back okay?" "I really need to sleep, but can I call you tomorrow to keep talking about this?"

## *be loving and supportive but don't make a big deal about it*

It's useful to try to keep your emotional level matching what they're giving out. If your emotions get bigger than theirs, they will feel they have to take care of you. Examples include: apologizing excessively for some affront, expressing a lot of outrage on their behalf, or responding to vulnerability with huge expressions of feeling and care.

You may love to get big bear hugs when you're crying, but your strong person might feel overwhelmed and smothered by it. Try starting smaller, like touching their hand or shoulder. Ask for permission to touch. Ask if they want a hug.

Let your strong person talk and try to listen with as little judgment and as much compassion as you can. Check in before giving advice to see if that's what they want, and be okay if they say no. You might offer observations and opinions if they're okay with it.

"Wow, that would really piss me off," is helpful empathy. "What the hell is wrong with that person!" might be too big and might feel to your strong person like you are centering your feelings and not interested in theirs. After a few rounds of this, you might be able to have a more free exchange of feelings, but be cautious the first time.

## accept dark humor

You and your rock can make liberal use of dark humor so long as it's clear that you emotionally understand where your rock is coming from and aren't judging or shaming them. Laughing with, and not at, is an important distinction.

If you're not into dark humor, understand that you may hear some of it and you don't have to laugh along but avoid criticizing it at the outset. Your strong person might be more sensitive to shame than you expect. Perhaps they hold themself to high standards and rarely give themself permission to be messy and ungracious.

Let them be messy for a while. Eventually you can bring in any needed accountability, and they will be more open to your opinion when they've processed.

## avoid talking about how much you admire their strength

Strong people may feel like their strength is a burden, that those around expect them to be superhuman and it's not okay to be weak and vulnerable. They might have been criticized in the past for being cold and "inhuman," which is even more painful.

If they are showing you vulnerability, this is an opportunity to let them know it's okay and you love them for being a whole person. Shifting the conversation back to how strong they are and how much you admire it may end up centering your feelings, minimizing their struggles, and communicating to them that their vulnerability is unacceptable.

Be strategic about saying, "You're being too hard on yourself." I can almost guarantee you they're being too hard on themself, they know it, they've been told it before, and probably feel a sense of embarrassment about it. Instead try fostering some curiosity about what in their life makes them feel like they have to be so hard on themself. What are they afraid will happen if they weren't strong all the time? That's where they need support.

## *make suggestions about steps for more support*

Strong people might be so used to taking care of their needs that when you ask "What can I do for you?" they will struggle to come up with any kind of answer at all. Sometimes your caring, effort, and presence will be more than enough. Sometimes they don't know how to assess their needs and name how others can support them.

You might ask some general questions about what they're dealing with and make some suggestions. If you're a person who is comfortable with receiving care and asking for what you want, this is an opportunity to use your experience to teach them. "Sometimes when I'm down it really makes me happy when people bring me a cooked meal. Could I do that for you?" Again, try not to personalize it if the person says no, defers, or doesn't have an answer for you. It's really not about how they feel about you, especially if you've made it to this point in the conversation.

### *apologize if needed*

If things don't go well and you realize you hurt their feelings, all is not lost. Your taking responsibility and offering a genuine apology may be quite healing for your strong person.

Knowing when to check in with your strong folks is a tricky thing. Think about what's been going on in their lives and how you would feel about it, then factor in that they might have the same feelings but be worse at acknowledging them, and act accordingly. Pay attention to if they seem more tired, forgetful, less gracious, more irritable, less on their game.

If there have been a lot of crises lately but things are starting to settle down, that is a great time. Often strong people learn to postpone their crisis response. When they know everyone's going to be okay or the worst is over, then they might allow themselves to have their crisis response, but struggle to acknowledge it since everyone else has moved on.

Thank you for taking the time to care for your strong people. They are more vulnerable than they want you to know.

# *in the midnight hour: on mattering, will, and hope*

My favorite bar in Chicago is a small brunch place in an out-of-the-way neighborhood that becomes a gay bar by night. One of its unique features is that, unlike most gay bars whose DJs provided meticulously curated playlists, this bar leaves a jar for song requests, which usually means that every time I go there's about an hour in the night where we're hearing songs we all know deeply and love well, shouting along to the lyrics. When we go back to visit, I make sure I make a stop there, and in August of 2019 I stood, grooving to Rihanna, and realized I wanted to hear "Like a Prayer" by Madonna.

A spiritual person who I followed on social media had posted a link to an astrological writing about the end of Jupiter's retrograde period and its return to direct motion. This writer, Aeolian Heart, spoke of Jupiter's role in faith, hope, and meaning, and in this article she used "Like a Prayer" as a love song between Spirit and Soul in their blissful union. From her perspective, Spirit is that part of us that animates and vitalizes us with a sense of larger purpose, a sense of meaning beyond what we can know in any moment. Soul, in turn, is closer to us, that part of us that gathers and processes our experiences and longings, both our sufferings and our joys, on this earth.

To say 2019 had been a rough year thus far would be accurate but almost laughably underwhelming, as it had begun to seem that every year since 2014 had been an increasing pile-up of collective nightmares. Personally, 2019 had featured a surprise palsy in my right hand which meant I was struggling to grip, lift, and type, and later the unexpected-in-the-moment collapse of a beloved relationship.

My old ways of being had come to fail me. My physical therapist had to teach me how to use my shoulders correctly so they weren't impinging the nerves in my arm. Meanwhile, all my efforts of people-pleasing and taking full accountability without insisting upon the same was no longer serving me or my partners, even when I convinced myself it was working fine. Physical and emotional stress eroded the resilience of my nervous system until one weird, unexpectedly fateful dinner in which I unconsciously massaged a sore spot in my upper arm and, according to my physical therapist, overtaxed the nerve until it finally had enough, as though giving up in self-protection.

That following month included three weeks in which my boyfriend and I had a fight nearly every day, or he somehow expressed ways in which I and our relationship was not working for him, and I saw my mental wellness plummeting. In the face of this, my anger rose with all the intensity of the long-submerged wants and needs that were no longer willing to be set aside for the comfort of others.

A clarity began to take me, that I needed to take full responsibility for my life and well-being, which at times meant becoming boundaried so that I could focus on caring for the needs that were not being included. When, finally, I decided I was not going to work harder than everyone else to keep things together, the relationship dissolved in that way that felt both sudden and yet, in retrospect, seemingly inevitable.

After this, meaning seemed to leave me for a time. What is meaning in a world in which everything eventually turns to dust? Beyond my personal turmoil, watching the rise of white supremacist fascists in the federal government, I had long recognized we were moving through a time of Fascism and resistance, but I'd found comfort in believing I could leave something for the future generations to connect with once the tide of authoritarianism failed and rolled back. But news of impending climate failure eroded my hope that there would even be future generations.

In the face of the most existential of existential dilemmas—the potential that our civilization, if not our species, could be in its final decline within my lifetime—I who had at times struggled with the depressive belief in the meaninglessness of my life now found even that familiar groove lacked comfort. In the past I found comfort in reincarnation and the hope of being born into a better future. Now I'd begun revisiting the belief in transcendence and the hope of leaving this hell world to a saner place. But none of these beliefs brought true comfort or meaning. They were, fundamentally, coming from a place of resignation and escape, not courage and liberation.

Reading the piece on Jupiter's direct station started to refresh that sense of hope. If only the hope for hope. And we were on vacation, and there was much dancing to be done, so when I stood in that bar screaming along to Whitney Houston asking if you wanted to dance with somebody who loves her, I realized that if I requested "Like a Prayer," not only was it likely we'd all dance to it, but we'd all be sharing this as a moment of ritual. And if my request was a spell for the restoration of hope, together we might call that energy forth.

As we sang, "In the midnight hour / I can feel your Power," late into the night I felt my will in manifestation. Here was an experience I wanted to have, and through my actions and intent I created it. My will was powerful.

And my will was a drop in the ocean. That moment was the confluence of a multitude of wills—all those who had shown up to dance and enjoy themselves, the workers who gave us libations and kept the space safe, the DJ who accepted and curated requests, the collective will of thousands upon thousands of people who have played "Like a Prayer" over the years such that the song has accreted depth and meaning, and of course Madonna herself who, with other musicians and producers and who knows who else created and launched this song into the world.

In Western occultism, will is a principle that is both practical and profoundly spiritual. It is our capacity to act in accordance with intention. To do the thing we say we will do. At its most grandiose, will becomes aligned with a sense of greater purpose and mission, a greater work that we are called to do that emerges from of a deep, persistent desire embedded throughout our lives. But there is not necessarily a way in which that greater will is superior to the simple, daily will, for the former is enhanced by the latter. Will is the expression of personal power by which we mark the world.

What is will in a world in which everything will turn to dust? We rarely if ever know the extent to which that mark changes the world, whether it was for good or ill or both, or how others are impacted. The lucky among us get glimpses of positive feedback.

I spent a good chunk of my early adulthood in Chicago, where I felt I didn't matter much. It was a story I'd brought with me out of my childhood, feeling invisible and unwanted and reactively distancing myself from all the people who may have liked and valued me a lot more than I knew at the time.

A story like that, "I don't matter," has an aliveness of its own that threads its way through time and space. It's tricky and adaptive, able to find new justification in any circumstance. In my childhood, I didn't matter because I couldn't play baseball or something like that, it's surprisingly hard to remember the specific circumstances outside of the felt memory of speaking and being ignored.

And as I write this, I remember all the times my parents urged me to speak up and stop mumbling. That is the other pernicious effect of such stories. By believing in their truth, we unwittingly participate in the conditions in which they are true.

In Chicago, I didn't matter because I wasn't very fit, my clothes weren't very nice, and I didn't have an impressive job. After leaving from college, where much of my identity was predicated on my grade point average, I did not know in what ground my Self could root and bloom. I spent a lot of time in bars where I saw guys who worked out a lot more extensively than I did and who either had the money or the willingness to go into debt for nicer clothes. I struggled in my early career ambitions. I didn't matter.

These days, when that automatic thought, "I don't matter," pops up, it wears different clothes. Now it may try to pass itself off as "woke," like, "No one cares what I have to say because I'm a cis white male." I write this to be honest, but I see it as a false story that entangles itself in privilege and aggrieved, self-pitying entitlement. Our 2016 presidential election showed that the privilege of cis white men can launch them into a job even with no experience in the field and proven failures in their previous career. Yet it's still what comes up in my head in moments where I feel tired, or vulnerable, or disconnected from my personal power.

A story like "I don't matter" seems persuasive when it's ricocheting off the interior of our skulls but makes no sense from the outside. The truth is, we matter. Our bodies are literally matter. Once we exist, our very existence is an influence upon the world. Having a body means I take up space, I consume resources that could go to others, I am participating in life and culture and relationships. If I am in a room, someone sees me, and my presence impacts them in a certain way. There is no opting out.

When we say, "I don't matter," I think often what we mean is more like, "I'm afraid other people don't consider me important or influential." "I don't matter" and its like may have been seeded by the people who didn't understand or know what to do with us when we were younger. Much of this is about social connection, power, respect, and status within groups and relationships. When other people persistently ignore, belittle, shame, minimize, neglect, or smother us, we begin to believe in the lie of our own unimportance. Then our bodies and energies start to embody what we fear we are.

I affect others. A room is not the same room when I am not in it. My friends and loved ones have different conversations when I am around versus when I am not. Everyone does. This is neither good nor bad. When I am alone with my best friend, our conversations are different from those we have when we're together with our partners, or at a table with a supervisor, or with a stranger.

If I show up feeling invisible, lonely, wounded, and desperate, my presence might draw others to try to connect with me or make them feel really uncomfortable about being around me. Usually a lot of that is about their previous experiences with other desperate, lonely people. If I show up feeling energized, kind, and full of life, my presence might create different experiences. I could have the same conversation differently based on my presence. I could bring up stories in other people.

We may feel unconscious as to how we want to matter, how much influence we have, unaware of how to use that influence with will. Influence is not wholly an inner trait, though developing our own power gives us greater influence and greater control over that influence. Personal power alone is not enough to undo centuries of racial propaganda that gives the voices of white people a bigger platform than others. What in part this means is that some people have to work much harder to cultivate an influence in alignment with their intention.

Madonna is a person who had to work harder than others because she has been a female pop singer in a male-dominated world, and a person whose platform was more accessible because she is a white woman in a white supremacist country. As much as I was drawn to her music as a kid and teenager, by my twenties I began to sense the calculation in her work and become more sensitized to the ways she appropriated the cultures and bodies of underground artists and people of color as adornments to promote her pop dominance. I'd become enamored of an idea of "depth," of a world of meaning beneath the surface that mere artifice could not touch, and Madonna is a master of artifice.

Now in my thirties I find myself spiraling back, sensing there is no essential meaning, no grand arbiter of what is worthy art and a worthy life and what is not, only creativity and power. We are the universe knowing itself, which today means to me that there is nothing intrinsically truer or better about my way of being and my aesthetic. Artifice that draws the attention and energy of millions accrues its own intensity of meaning, its own power. I could work for years on a poem that I consider perfectly wrought and die having it unread, whereas simply requesting "Like a Prayer" at a club created an experience of wholeness and unity among folks who likely would be fighting with each other later that night.

All of this dances around hope. To act as though one's will matters and has meaning in a world in which everything turns to dust is to embody hope. Yet hope is as likely to defeat us as to empower us. Without hope, some of us feel depleted and fall into a sense of despondency. Others of us see hope as a luxury afforded only to those who have never truly endured trauma and failure. Yet even those whose lives are constant battle, without hope, may sense that giving up the fight for dignity would be a greater death.

Too many of us are hoping and letting that hope get us off the hook. In the face of tyranny, mass incarceration, and climate change we hope someone will do something. Then we need not feel inconvenient feelings about not doing anything. So we don't have to take a risk and suffer consequences of that. We need to start looking to see who is doing the work, and supporting them. And if no one is doing the work, it may be ours to do.

We want hope to hinge upon knowing our efforts matter, but we do not know how to measure it. How we measure that, typically, is by what we call "success," and in a capitalist economy "success" means sales, numbers, recognition, status. But success could be measured in many other ways. Success could be whether it brings ease to another person, or connects with another. Success could be simply feeling more alive and purposeful. Success could be the synchronicities that arise, the approval of the gods. Success could be the accomplishment of a goal, no matter how small.

It is the way of things for life to grow, flourish, die, decompose, and become another kind of life. There are people and ancestors who remain alive within me, who animate me with gifts and wounds, inspiration and teachings. And there are people who once mattered very much to me—friends, lovers with whom I was passionately embroiled—who are no longer in my life. At the time of the breakup or loss, this is a horrifying thought. After so much beauty, intensity, passion, connection, it hurts to imagine all those colors will eventually bleach like a picture that's been left out in the light too long. Yet memory, feeling, and meaning continues to change. Even what has been closed and lost may continue to evolve. The future may change our experience of the past, and what was long past may re-emerge to shift the future.

My feelings and nature evolves in a spiral pattern, coiling around core issues that continue to deepen and expand. First I adored Madonna, then I critiqued and distanced myself from her, then I grudgingly returned to the pleasure I took in her music with the recognition of how much comes from my own Self, my own meaning meeting hers. When I was younger, I heard in her a voice of erotic liberation, authenticity, and emotional depth. Perhaps that is true of her, and perhaps she is also a skilled opportunist who knows how to make money and use people and resources to stay relevant. All of this can coexist within the same body.

Indeed, Madonna represents to me a well-honed capacity of will. Not only does she act as though she matters, she seems to insist upon it. In spite of all the critiques that would have slowed me down, made me reflect and doubt my voice, she continues her efforts of taking exciting new musical trends and making them pop-friendly for her own success. It seems that she has continued the work she set out to do—to make pop music and be famous.

Will that plows forward, heedless of the damage it causes, is what makes toxic our oceans and heats up our planet, harms and splits our communities without accountability. It is the relentless pursuit of profit at all costs, without humility, without consideration, without receiving and blending with the will of community. There are psychological benefits in asserting one's ego at any cost, in putting one's interests ahead of everyone else's, but there are also psychological benefits to having healthy, meaningful, loving relationships. The success of a strong relationship depends upon our willingness to accept each other's influence, to take each other seriously. And at the same time we need to be clear in our own truth.

In the book *Active Hope,* Joanna Macey and Chris Johnstone define a practice of "active hope" as "becoming active participants in bringing about what we hope for." Rather than passively wishing for something to occur, for people to behave differently, active hope is the blending of will and desire to become what we seek. Through embodying the hope and virtue we desire, too, we experience that conflict between Spirit and Soul. Spirit calls upon me to express virtue in the world, to dignify myself and others, to do the work before me with a grateful heart, and to suffer change and transformation for the survival of what I love. Within the realm of Soul, my parts experience the pleasures and pains of this experience and emerge in conflict and questioning, testing and refining these virtues.

If my hoped-for virtues are to be kind, accountable, and honest, and I am in relationship with a person who does not practice these in the way or to the extent that I do, then I begin to experience a conflict in my soul. Parts of me concerned with fairness and my own needs act out when I repeatedly concede to the valid points of the other person while feeling no concession to my own. To deny these hurts and unmet needs is the path of spiritual bypassing, choosing Spirit above all else and holding more and more rigidly to that path, in which case virtues eventually become dry and tyrannical. Too much light that makes the land a desert.

Yet to release my Spirit and wholly invest myself in the conflicting needs of my Soul may lead me into too much darkness, the watery depths in which I can find no ground. A part of me wants desperately to do what it takes to keep the relationship going. A part of me feels disappointed, deceived, and hurt. A part of me says if I could only be calmer, more centered, stronger, then we could work through it. A part of me feels exhausted and resentful, telling the story that I always have to be the bigger person and it's unfair. And all of these parts have validity. They all emerge from the situation, and they all have deep roots in pains and compromises I made years ago to make sense of the world and survive. In a sense, if I let any of these parts choose my path, that path would become my truth. Yet the other truths would not dissolve, they would continue to fester and make me more tense, more sensitive, more reactive, less generous, more disingenuous.

Spirit and Soul pass through the filters of personal and collective belief, all the various meanings we've gathered through education and experience, and then they touch in the human heart. What I thought was kindness, accountability, and honesty are not invalid but there was a flaw in understanding, a bias informed by my fears of losing my loved one. I had not been kind, accountable to, or honest with myself about what I am willing to accept and how hard I am willing to work. Even with all my work on integrity, I was taken aback by how much I tried to keep threatening feelings at bay—to essentially deny their mattering—until they demanded reckoning.

What is hope in a world in which everything turns to dust? Pema Chödron writes about generative hopelessness in *When Things Fall Apart*: "Giving up hope is encouragement to stick with yourself, not to run away, to return to the bare bones, no matter what's going on. If we totally experience hopelessness, giving up all hope of alternatives to the present moment, we can have a joyful relationship with our lives, an honest, direct relationship that no longer ignores the reality of impermanence and death."

From Chödron's perspective as a Buddhist, hope is the experience of attachment and aversion that keeps us constantly restless, constantly seeking escape from the present moment and thus imprisoned by our inability to tolerate what is. Hope is the constant adjustment of posture in sitting meditation instead of being with whatever arises. Hope is the constant avoiding of living one's life by believing if we can hold on things will be better in a few years.

Passive hope is neither empowering nor interesting. It is a state in which the Soul hopes someone else gets the Spirit to act so that it does not have to experience its own evolution. Active hope is everything. Active hope is aliveness, using my mattering intentionally to affect the mattering of those around me. Active hope is showing up to the action, even if I'm only one body among many, adding my will and energy to the collective work. Active hope is the descent of Spirit to enliven and direct us, to find the deepest wishes of the Soul and to begin to live them through in the world that we have. It is not a magical skipping over of pain, suffering, or effort. Effort is what makes space for Spirit amidst the glory of the Soul. There is no one coming to save us. We're what we've got.

www.ingramcontent.com/pod-product-compliance
Ingram Content Group UK Ltd.
Pitfield, Milton Keynes, MK11 3LW, UK
UKHW020414250726
13967UKWH00007B/2638

9 781735 794426